Introduction to Journalism

James Glen Stovall

First Inning Press

in conjunction with

the

Intercollegiate Online News Network

This book is part of the

Tennessee Journalism Séries

© 2012 James Glen Stovall

Table of Contents

Forward

Journalism is an exciting adventure, not just a way to make a living.

Our hope for this book is that it can convey to students some of the excitement and the importance of journalism to society.

This will be the first of several ebooks planned for the high school journalism student. They are produced with the thought in mind that the world needs well-trained, committed, honest journalism to help us face the future.

Introduction to Journalism — a first look into the field of journalism — is written and produced for teachers and students who are looking ahead, not for those who are hoping that somehow the past will return.

Journalism today is being practiced in an environment that is vastly different from the one journalists knew in the early 1990s. The engine that has driven that change, of course, is the information technology that we all use, specifically the Internet and the World Wide Web. Where print and broadcasting were once the chief technologies of journalism and the media in which journalism could be presented, they are now secondary tools and are fading in importance.

This book is for the people who are willing to embrace the journalism of the future and who are brave enough to leave the pack and lead their students into this world. Teachers who step out into the future and form news websites for their students to learn and practice on or who require their students to use blogs, Twitter, Facebook and other modern tools of communication and information presentation are the ones for whom this book is written.

They are also the ones to whom this book is dedicated.

Special thanks here is due to Edward Henczel, an instructors in the Department of Journalism at Langara

College in Vancourver, BC, Canda, for proof-reading and early edition of this book.

Tennessee Journalism Series

The **Tennessee Journalism Series** is a set of texts and instructional material developed by the faculty of the University of Tennessee School of Journalism and Electronic Media for journalism students and instructors around the world.

The idea behind the series is "multimedia first." That is, these books are built for the iPad and contain a variety of multimedia elements: text, audio, video, photo galleries, interactive images, and interactive reviews and quizzes.

At present, nine books are available on iBookstore for download to the iPad:

- **Feature Writing**

- **Going Online: How to Start a Scholastic News Website**

- **How to Get a Job as an On-Air TV Journalist (Denae D'Arcy)**

- **Introduction to Journalism**

- **Media Reporting**

- **Photojournalism: Telling Stories with Pictures and Words**

- **Reporting: An Introduction**

- The First Amendment

- Writing Like a Journalist (Jim Stovall)

Other books in active development include:
A. Journalism and Social Media (Ioana Coman and Margaret Grigsby)

B. Legal Issues for Journalism Students (Mike Martinez and Dwight Teeter)

C. The British Media (Mark Harmon)

Full descriptions of the books available with their iBookstore, Kindle and Amazon links can be found at http://tnjnseries.com.

What is Journalism

Journalism is a vital profession for the health and operation of a democratic society. People need to be informed about what is happening around them. In addition, people want news. Journalists are people trained to witness important events in society and tell people about those events.

1. Definitions

Purpose
To help students learn and understand the basic elements of journalism.

Importance
Journalism is defined by its history, concepts and practices. Students should understand the role, importance and limits of journalism in our society. The elements and concepts introduced in this section – and the way in which they fit together – form the basis for everything else that the student will learn in this course on journalism.

Journalism is one of the formal means by which a society learns about itself. It creates a common pool of information and knowledge that allows the society to be cohesive, to assess its strengths and weaknesses, and to make life better for its individual members.

Imagine a society without news and a free flow of information.

It's almost impossible to do because the very nature of our social interactions are based on shared information and shared values.

What is the first thing you do when you enter the school building in the morning? Without realizing it, you look around to see if anything has changed since you saw it last. You listen to what people are saying. You share information and thoughts you have with friends and those around you.

You talk about what? A history test? A football game? A new teacher? Something a fellow student has said?

All of these and a thousand other topics are the "news" that you encounter in your school every day. Some topics and information may be trivial. Others may be of utmost importance. As you go through the day, you continue to gather and share information. In doing so, you are acting as your own journalist within the school environment – gathering and sharing information that you believe is important or interesting.

What you do individually every day at school or work or anywhere else you are, journalism seeks to do on a larger scale for society. It gathers information, processes it and distributes it to a wide audience. We will be examining many of the details of how this happens in this course of study.

Meanwhile, here are a few definitions that will help us get started:

Journalism – the process of gathering news and information and distributing it to audiences through various media.

News – events and subjects that meet certain criteria or "news values" (see Chapter 2 News) such as impact, currency, timeliness and prominence.

Reporting – the process of gathering information by journalists.

News organization – a company that is devoted to the process and products of journalism.

Medium (plural: media) – the means through which information is distributed to a broader audience. In journalism, media include newspapers, magazines, radio, television, and the web.

Style – rules governing writing and usage of words in journalism.

Professionalism – the culture and self-imposed rules governing the conduct of journalists in the process of gathering and reporting news.

Public service – the idea that journalists do not serve particular individuals, groups or interests in society but rather have a wider responsibility to society as a whole.

Ask yourself:
A. Who in your family is most interested in the news and in current events? What sources of information does that person use?

B. List the important things that you have learned or that you have thought of in studying this. Try to write them in very short but complete sentences. Now make an audio file of those points so that you can download it onto your iPod or MP3 player.

Summary
Journalism is necessary for society to function properly.

Journalism is conducted by people trained to do so, and news and information is distributed through formal organizations called the news media.

The idea of journalists having a "public service" mission is an important one.

News helps keep society dynamic and interesting.

References
Reeves, Richard. What People Know: Freedom of the Press. Cambridge, MA: Harvard University Press, 1999.

Stovall, James Glen. Journalism: Who, What, When, Where, Why and How. Boston: Allyn and Bacon, 2006.

JPROF.com, http://jprof.com

Poynter Institute, http://poynter.org

Advanced reading material

Klaidman, Stephen and Tom L. Beauchamp. The Virtuous Journalist. New York: Oxford University Press, 1987.

Fallows, James. Breaking the News: How the Media Undermine American Democracy. New York: Pantheon, 1995.

Fry, Don, ed. Believing the News. St. Petersburg: Poynter Institute for Media Studies, 1985.

Review questions

What is news?

events and subjects that meet certain criteria or "news values"

anything that might happen in a given day

anything you might be interested in

anything the government says you should be interested in

The process of gathering information so that it can be distributed through a news medium:

announcing

shifting

reporting

administering

What do journalists call the standard rules of writing?

penmanship

fashion

takes

style

One of the formal means by which a society tells itself about itself is

entertainment

school

government

journalism

Medium is a singular now; its plural is

media

mediums

mediate

meds

2. News

Purpose
To introduce students to the concept of news as the most important product of journalism.

Importance
News is the most important product of journalism. All of the efforts of journalists are directed toward producing accounts of news events and topics that are accurate, precise, clear and efficient.

News is information that is interesting and important to a significant audience of news consumers. One of the jobs of the journalist – and journalism in general – is to select those events and topics that should be reported on. One of the factors that journalists consider in this select is whether or not the event or the topic will make a difference in people's lives.

News should do at least one of three things: inform, entertain and persuade. It may do all three.

The most important function of news is to inform. Journalists do not often concern themselves with what individuals may do with the information the journalists report. News consumers may use it for good or ill. The important thing for the journalist is that society be informed about what is going on within its ranks. One of the basic tenets of modern society is that people have information on which to make decisions about their lives. Journalists feel that one of their main jobs is to contribute to that pool of information.

Much that is in the news media, however, does not make a significant difference in our lives. The comings and goings of celebrities, for instance, or the scores from Saturday's football games do little to influence the decisions about how we live our lives. This illustrates the second function of news: to entertain. The entertainment function is not a trivial one. It enriches our lives by feeding our interests and interactions.

A third function of news is to persuade. This concept has a larger meaning than simply convincing us to go out and buy a tube of toothpaste or a new car. The word we should be using is acculturation. By telling us what happens in our society, news helps individuals find their place in that society. It informs us about a common set of attitudes and values that many of the individuals in society share. It also shows us how those attitudes and values play out in our lives.

This is not to say that everyone in society thinks in the same way or share a common set of political or religious believes. We certainly do not. In fact, one of the common characteristics about all modern society is its diversity – the fact that a society can function with many individuals believing very different things and coming from backgrounds that are wide-ranging. Yet, we all share a basic respect for the sovereignty of the individual, the political and legal system, and the importance of honest and civil behavior. News helps to reinforce and strengthen that respect.

News helps keep society dynamic and interesting. Variety, as the old saying goes, is the spice of life. Actually, variety in our lives is more than spice. It is a necessary ingredient to a modern and creative society. By adding to that variety with current information, news helps us identify problems and possibilities that need to be solved or exploited. News shows how other people are acting and thinking – people with whom we may have no contact otherwise. News expands our horizons and helps us to see beyond our immediate and local situations.

Journalism and what it produces – news – is thus an important part of the life of the society as well as the life of the individual. In the previous section (1.1 Definitions) we discussed the "public service" aspect of journalism, something you may want to review. The fact that news contributes to the proper functioning of society is the underlying reason why many people – and possibly you – feel the call to the profession of journalism.

News values

Journalists use the following criteria, commonly referred to as "news values," to determine whether or not an event or topic is worthy of attention by the news media:

Impact. How many people does the event affect? How widespread and long-lasting is this affect?

Timeliness. How recently did the event occur?

Prominence. Important and well-known people make news, sometimes even when they are doing normal, everyday things. If the president takes his kids to an ice cream parlor, that's likely to catch the attention of journalists.

Proximity. The closer to home an event is, the most likely it is to become news. A car accident would not be news if it occurred 50 miles away, but if it occurred in the downtown of your home town, it would be more likely to get coverage.

Conflict. Opposing ideas or people are likely to create conflict, and journalists believe that conflict is one of the things that people are most interested in. Conflict can be violence in the street or in more civil settings such as legislative debates or courtrooms.

Currency. Events and topics about current ideas and things already in the news are likely to receive news coverage.

Unusualness. When something truly out of the ordinary occurs – say, an 80-year-old great-grandmother gets her college degree – it is more likely to become news.

Summary

• News is information that is interesting and important to a significant audience of news consumers.

• News should do at least one of three things: inform, entertain and persuade.

• By telling us what happens in our society, news helps individuals find their place in that society.

• News helps keep society dynamic and interesting.

Ask yourself:
A. What are the things that are most important for you to know (information) from the news media in making the important decisions in your life?

B. What are the things that you are most interested in (entertainment), and what do you find out about them from the news media?

C. What are the things that people should learn as they grow up or as they immigrate into society (persuasion), and what can they learn about them from the news media?

References and readings
Kovach, Bill and Tom Rosenstiel. The Elements of Journalism. New York: Crown Publishers, 2001.

Stovall, James Glen. The Complete Editor. Boston: Allyn and Bacon, 2005.

Stovall, James Glen. Journalism: Who, What, When, Where, Why and How. Boston: Allyn and Bacon, 2006.

Cappella, Joseph N. and Kathleen Hall Jamieson. Spiral of Cynicism: The Press and the Public Good. New York: Oxford University Press, 1997.

Fuller, Jack. News Values. Chicago: University of Chicago Press, 1996.

Review questions

What is meant by the impact of an event?

when it happens

how many people it effects

the important people involved

whether it's national or international

What does the news value of currency mean?

ideas and issues being discussed now

ideas and issues that are of interest to others, but no necessarily you

basic principles of society

only political ideas

The most important function of news is to

entertain

persuade

inform

dictate

3. News Consumers

Purpose
To define the term "news consumers" and to help students understand the role that the audience plays in the production and dissemination of news.

Importance
The audience is an increasingly important part of the product and process of journalism. Understanding the role of the audience is vital to understanding the way journalism works.

Less than 50 years ago, most people in the United States had rather limited access to the news media compared to today. Most places had at most two newspapers, but a typical household would only subscribe to one. There might be a half a dozen to a dozen radio stations that could be easily picked up during the day. A well-populated area would have three local television stations, each affiliated with one of the three major networks (ABC, NBC, and CBS). In some areas, all of these stations would have local news operations, but that was not the case everywhere.

The three major networks produced news shows from which most Americans got their daily news. These shows lasted 30 minutes and were broadcast once a day. Local television stations had news shows lasting 30 minutes that were broadcast twice a day. There was no CNN and no 24-hour news (except for a few radio stations in very large cities).

And the audience did not matter very much.

That's because the news media (journalists) made two assumptions about the audience. One was that the audience was a "mass audience." That is, the only really important thing about the audience was how large it was. Getting larger audiences (more newspaper subscribers, more television viewers, etc.) was the only thing that really mattered. The second assumption was that the audience for news would be there because they had no choice. The number of news outlets they had access to was very limited.

These assumptions led many journalists to believe that the preferences of individuals within the audience did not matter very much. As long as the news organizations produced news and information about a number of different topics, they could retain this mass audience.

This is the media environment in which your grandparents grew up.

How things have changed.

The changes began in the 1970s when cable television, once meant for the rural areas that could not receive an over-the-air signal, began to spread into the cities. With cable came a growing number of "channels" that were not affiliated with the major television networks. In 1980, the Cable News Network (CNN) was launched as the first 24-hour news channel. The number of news channels grew steadily through the 1980s.

This led to the concept of the "segmented audience," as opposed to the mass audience we mentioned earlier. Many of these new cable channels were not trying to reach everyone. Rather, they wanted people with special interests in sports, business, food, homes, gardening, etc.

The most profound change came in the 1990s with the Internet and the World Wide Web. By the mid-1990s, it was obvious to many people that the web was going to change just about everything about the discipline and process of journalism.

The biggest change would be the relationship that journalists would have with their audiences. No longer could journalists serve up whatever news they wanted to produce and be confident the audience would buy it. The audience had too many choices. Now journalists had to pay much closer attention to what members of the audience wanted and had to respond to the audience in a very different way. They had to let the audience in on the process of journalism – something they had never done before – and the audience became active participants in the process.

Journalism changed from producing "news as product" to producing "news as conversation." That change is still occurring.

How much does the audience pay attention to news?

Here's one example: the swine flu outbreak in 2009. The Pew Center for People and the Press conducted a survey asking people where they got their information about swine flu. The results of the survey showed that people heard about the swine flu from a variety of sources: local television news (69%), cable news channels (63%), nightly network news (53%), the Internet (49%), and newspapers (48%). The survey went on to ask people what source was the "most useful," and here is what the survey report said about the results:

But the rankings change when people are asked which source has been most useful in learning about the global outbreak that started in Mexico. One quarter cite the internet, 19% name the cable news networks and 17% their local television news. About one-in-ten cite the nightly network newscasts or newspapers (9% each).

Read the summary of the survey report here:

http://people-press.org/report/514/local-tv-a-top-source-for-swine-flu-news

What does all this say about the audience for news?

Summary
• Two generations ago, journalists and the news media thought of audiences as "mass audiences" for the most part.

• One of the biggest changes in journalism in the past two generations has been "audience segmentation."

• The web has brought the audience much closer to the journalistic process and has changed the concept of "news as product" to "news as conversation."

Discussion:

A. Think about your typical day. What are the news organizations where you regularly get your news? Make a list and order that list from "receive most news" to "receive least news."

B. What types of news are you interested in – politics, music, sports, local entertainment, etc.?

C. What do you think is meant by the concept of "news as conversation"? That concept is not explained in this section but will be dealt with later. Still, you might give it some thought and see what your fellow students think about it.

Projects
A. Interview a fellow student, one who is not part of the journalism course, about what news they are interested in and what news organizations they pay attention to. Make a list of these organizations, and during a discussion about this topic, share what you have learned with fellow class members.

B. The content portion of this section talks about how people paid attention to the swine flu outbreak in 2009. What is the biggest piece of medical news that has occurred as you read this? Ask some students where they got their information about this story.

References
Pew Center for People and the Press, Local TV A Top Source For Swine Flu News, May 6, 2009

http://people-press.org/report/514/local-tv-a-top-source-for-swine-flu-news

James Glen Stovall, Web Journalism: Practice and Promise of a New Medium, Allyn and Bacon, 2004.

JPROF.com, http://jprof.com

Advanced reading material

Readership Institute - The Institute is based at the Media Management Center at Northwestern University.

http://www.readership.org/

The State of the News Media - An annual report on American journalism.

http://www.stateofthenewsmedia.org

Clark, Roy Peter and Cole C. Campbell. The Values and Craft of American Journalism. Gainesville: University Press of Florida, 2002.

Review questions

In the last 50 years, what's changed about the audience for journalists?

Not very much

The audience for news is much smaller than it used to be.

Journalists have to consider the audience much more than they used to.

Audiences are much more hostile to journalists than they used to be.

The most profound thing that happened to the mass media in the 1990s was the development of cable TV

the cellphone

the development of the web

the OJ Simpson trial

Journalism has changed from producing "news as product" to

producing "news as conversation."

de-segmenting audiences.

producing "news as persuasion."

4. Professional Values

Purpose
Basic concepts and shared values support the profession of journalism. Students should have these concepts and values in their minds as they begin to learn the practices of the journalist.

Importance
Professional values define the field of journalism and explain why it differs from other activities, jobs and professions.

Journalists generally agree that they are on a mission to find the truth. Not The Truth. That's the job of philosophers and theologians. Rather, what journalists are after is the everyday truth, or truths, that have an impact on our lives.

The mission of seeking the truth about our lives – facts, context, points of view, etc. – determines both the attitudes and the processes by which journalists work. We will discuss some of the most important of these in this section and group them under the general heading of "professional values."

One of the most important of these professional values is the seeking of accurate information — or more succinctly, accuracy. Journalists see themselves as observers of their society, trying not to take sides in a controversy but rather acting as independent witnesses. By the very nature of gathering information and observing human interactions, they must often make interpretations and judgments. But they consider these judgments secondary to their really important job, which is to uncover information and present it to an audience in an interesting and understandable form.

As such, one of the professional values that is highly important to the journalist is verification of information. Verification means that information comes from the most expert and reliable sources and that it can be generally agreed upon within that circle of sources. We will devote much more attention to the concept and process of verification in a later section of this course.

Another value of the journalist is fairness. The journalist recognizes that life is full of conflict, opposing ideas and differing points of view. Sometimes these differences are minor and of little consequence. Sometimes they are enormous and create violent conflict among people or groups. The journalist, as much as possible, tries to weigh differing opinions and points of view sympathetically and rationally. The journalist tries to see an event or idea without having a personal interest. This is not always easy. Journalists are not only human but they are also individuals within a society. They join groups, they have friends and families, and they have attitudes about right and wrong as everyone else does. Journalists recognize their own foibles when they are in the process of doing journalism.

From these efforts flows the idea of independence. Journalists, and the organizations for which they work, should not be dependent on the individuals or organizations they cover. While many news organizations accept advertising revenues as a means of economic survival, they try not to let advertisers influence the type of news coverage they give events and ideas. Journalists are generally forbidden to accept gifts or things of value from those people they are covering.

The idea of public service (which we discussed in 1.1 Definitions) is an important part of the way journalists see themselves and their work. Journalists work very hard. The hours are often long and the tasks frustrating. Generally, they do not make a lot of money (although one can, as a journalist, make a very good living). What drives journalists is not the thought of making a lot of money, achieving high status or an easy lifestyle. Rather, it is the idea that journalists can contribute to making society better – giving people information they can use to make good decisions about their own lives, uncovering the wrongs that may be occurring in society or contributing to the marketplace of ideas.

Competitiveness is another value of journalists, although it is one that is never discussed very much. Journalists like to be first with information they present to their audiences. That's called "breaking a story," and when a journalist and news organization breaks an important story, they take enormous pride in doing so. This drive for "bragging rights," if you will, is highly important within the profession, although it is one that journalists do not discuss publicly very much because they believe that their audiences are not terribly interested.

In this sense, journalists share a respect for others in their profession and for the general values and practices of the profession. But they do not always agree about the particulars of those practices or about how other journalists act. Debates among journalists about those values and practices are taking place constantly.

To get an idea of some of those debates, listen to the radio program On the Media (http://onthemedia.org). You will hear journalists commenting on and critiquing the work of other journalists and trying to discover the best ways to practice their profession.

In the next section, we will discuss some of the personal attributes that it takes to become a journalist. Have you got what it takes?

Summary
• Journalists generally share a set of "professional values" that help distinguished journalism from other professions.

• These professional values include a devotion to finding truthful information, verification, fairness, a sense of public service, independence, competitiveness, and a general respect for others in the profession.

• Journalists engage in continuous and lively debates about their values and their practices – something that makes the professional dynamic and interesting.

Project:
Which of the professional values that are discussed in this section are the most important? (As a classroom exercise, the class should be divided into groups, and

each group should be given one of the professional values. They should be given time to research it and then make the case for it as being important.)

Discussion:
A. Why is public service listed as a professional value? What the author says about it gives some of the reasons. Are there others that you can think of or others that you can discover after doing some research on the topic?

B. After reading this section, how do you think journalism differs from other professions? If you have a family member who is a doctor or lawyer, ask them about the "professional values" of that profession and compare them to what is in this section.

References
Itule, Bruce D. and Douglas A. Anderson. News Writing and Reporting for Today's Media, 6th ed. Boston: McGraw-Hill, 2003.

Lewis, Anthony, editor. Written into History: Pulitzer Prize Reporting of the Twentieth Century from the New York Times. New York: Times Books, 2001.

Harrington, Walt. Intimate Journalism: The Art and Craft of Reporting Everyday Life. Thousand Oaks, CA: Sage Publications, 1997.

Review questions

One of the most important professional values for journalists is

being able to take good pictures

speaking a foreign language fluently

gathering accurate information

making sure all your friends know how hard you work

What does "independence" mean in terms of professional journalistic values?

the right of the journalist to report whatever he or she wants

the separation of the journalist and the news organization from the events or issues they are covering

the separation of the news organization from the journalists who are working for it

5. Personal Attributes

Purpose
Students should take away two ideas from this module:
one, an understanding of the personal attributes that
help make a successful journalist; and two, a sense of
how those attributes can be developed.

Importance
Journalists are special people. Not everyone has what it
takes to become a journalist. The attributes for being a
successful journalist can be developed by those who are
willing to work at it.

Many people try to become journalists, but not everyone
succeeds.

Some people find the work too hard and the hours too
long. Others get frustrated at having to find information
and persuade people to give it to them. Some realize that
they do not have the competitive fire to survive in the
work of journalism. Still others discover that they do not
have the skills to be a good writer, reporter or editor.

Yet, many other people do become journalists and find
the work rewarding. And a growing number of young
people are taking an interest in the profession.

So what does it take to become a good journalist?

In the previous section (1.4 Professional values), we
discussed some of the values and attitudes that those in
the profession share as they do their journalistic work.
This section presents some of the personal attributes –
the things that an individual needs to bring to their
professional work.

The first and foremost personal attribute is a strong and
confident sense of personal integrity. In a word: honesty.
Journalists must be honest about themselves and their
place in the world. They must understand their own
biases and admit to them. They must act professionally

and in ways that enhance their credibility. As seekers after truth, they must be themselves truthful.

Developing high personal standards of conduct are essential for the journalist. They must be able to defend not only what they produce – their articles and reports – but also the way in which those reports are produced.

Another attribute of the journalist is a wide-ranging curiosity about the world. Journalists should want to know the what, why and how of many things. They should be willing to listen to people tell their stories and express their opinions without being judgmental about them. They should have the ability to ask questions that not only get information but also show their sources they are genuinely interested in the topic being discussed.

Young people who want to enter the professional of journalism should be wide and voracious readers. They should always have a stack of books and magazines that they are trying to get through. They should explore deeply the subjects they are taking in their high school curriculum, reading well beyond the textbook assignments.

One of the most insidious reasons for not pursuing a topic or subject cited by high school students (and others) is: "That will never be of any use to me." That kind of thinking is wrong on many levels, but it is deathly limiting to people who want to become journalists. Simply put, a journalist should know as much about as many things as possible.

A skill that all potential journalists should have is the ability to use the language – particularly the ability to write – and an interest in developing that skill. All journalists must write, and they must edit what they and others write. That means, first, knowing the generally accepted rules of grammar, spelling, punctuation and diction and being able to apply those rules to their writing. Second, journalists should understand the meanings of words and how they are used in the context of writing and speaking.

Beyond these technical aspects of writing, journalists should enjoy the writing process and should derive some satisfaction from it. Some people do not like to write. It is difficult, and they get little satisfaction from doing it. Fair enough. But these are people who would not do well in journalism. The expectation of the profession is that people who attempt to be journalists should be able to write and should not mind doing so.

(If you think you would like to go into journalism but don't think that you write well enough to do so, don't worry. You can improve you skills, and you will have many opportunities to do so.)

Another attribute that is helpful to journalists is the ability and willingness to work hard. Journalism sometimes requires long hours. It can be frustrating. Journalists cannot make people talk with them or give them information. They cannot make people return their phone calls or answer their emails. Journalists have to learn to live with these frustrations.

In addition, all news organizations have deadlines and work must be produced by these deadlines. This can lead to a great amount of tension as a deadline approaches, and a journalist has to learn to absorb these pressures and produce high quality work in a short amount of time. In addition, a journalist must be willing to accept criticism of his or her work. The work the journalist does is, we hope, seen by a large audience. Inevitably, that work will not please everyone in the audience, and the journalist has to understand and accept that. Journalists are not always highly regard, but they have to believe in what they do and work hard at it despite being criticized or under-appreciated.

The best journalists have well developed analytical abilities. Sometimes these are described as "thinking skills." Journalists can put disparate facts together, making connections and drawing conclusions. Most of all, they do not mind questioning what people tell them. They are not afraid to put information to the test of checks and double-checks, of research, of asking independent sources.

A lot of what is described in the previous paragraph can be defined by one word: skepticism. Journalists are skeptical about what they see and hear. They want to hear from a second source. They want to analyze and think about what others tell them. They are unwilling to simply accept an assertion at face value.

A journalist's skepticism should not degenerate into cynicism (disbelieving everything anyone says). Nor should it make the journalist obnoxious or uncivil. But journalists should not allow civility to stop them from asking difficult, embarrassing or uncomfortable questions if the need arises.

All of the attributes and skills discussed in this section help the journalist do his or her job. They are skills that are valued by the profession and are expected of those who want to practice journalism for a living.

Summary
• A journalist must have a strong sense of honesty and personal integrity.

• Journalists must be able to write well. With the changing media environment, they must also develop their ability to speak clearly.

• Being skeptical – questioning even the most obvious things – is part of the journalist's intellectual makeup.

Ask yourself:
A. Consider all of the personal attributes discussed in this section. Which of those do you already possess? Which would you have to develop if you were going to become a journalist?

B. As you continue through this course, one of the personal attributes you will be asked to develop is your skill in using the language. How good are you at using the language now in writing and speaking? Where are your weaknesses? Strengths?

Discussion:
A. Why is honesty the number 1 personal attribute the author identifies for being a journalist? Do you think that most journalists live up to this attribute?

B. Read a news story that refers to several different sources of information. What were the analytical abilities of the necessary for the journalist to put that story together?

References

Stepp, Carl Sessions. Writing As Craft and Magic. Boston: McGraw-Hill, 2000.

Brooks, Brian S., George Kennedy, Daryl R. Moen and Don Ranly. Telling the Story: Writing for Print, Broadcast and Online Media. New York: Bedford/St. Martins, 2001.

Stovall, James Glen. Journalism: Who, What, When, Where, Why and How. Boston: Allyn and Bacon, 2006.

JPROF.com, http://jprof.com

Poynter Institute, http://poynter.org

Advanced reading material

Society of Professional Journalists

http://spj.org

Newsthinking.com - Bob Baker from the Los Angeles Times maintains this site.

http://www.newsthinking.com/

Adam, G. Stuart and Roy Peter Clark. Journalism: The Democratic Craft. New York: Oxford University Press, 2005.

Ross, Lillian. Reporting Back: Notes on Journalism. Washington, DC: Counterpoint, 2002.

Review questions

The ability to work hard

is not something journalists have to do

is a highly prized personal attribute of journalists

is something that journalists are born with

The most important personal characteristic of a journalist is

honesty

the ability to work hard

curiosity

intelligence

If you are going to be a journalist, one of the things you have to do is

be an expert in Facebook

understand scientific values

read voraciously and widely

6. Journalism Today

Purpose
• To impress upon students that change is a part of the field of journalism and has been a constant in the history of journalism.

• The changes taking place in journalism today are affecting the economics of journalism, and the future is as yet unsettled.

Importance
Journalism has always been a dynamic field and never more so than today. Changes in journalism have often been driven by breakthroughs in technology. This is a basic characteristic of the field that students should understand.

The world does not lack for mass media, news organizations, or journalism. Plenty of news fills printed pages, the broadcast airwaves, and the World Wide Web. News organizations large and small abound. Hundreds of thousands of people make their living as journalists or in helping to produce this news. Others do not work at it full time but contribute to today's news environment.

But there are those who fear that it will not always be.

That's because of the dramatic changes that have taken place in the field of journalism in the last two decades.

Those two decades have seen the fracturing of television audiences and a dramatic growth in the number of television channels that produce and broadcast news. More frightening to many people has been the decline in the number and economic stability of newspapers.

At the end of the last century, newspapers were giant organizations and highly profitable. A strong single newspaper dominated the news environment of a city or geographic area and produced most of its journalism.

These newspapers would employ many journalists and perform many of the functions of journalism that we have discussed in the other modules of this section.

But during the 1990s – particularly the last half of the decade – this environment began to change. The major cause of this change was the Internet and the increasing access to broadband connections in the work and home environment. The growing popularity of the World Wide Web as a source for news made it the preferred medium because of its immediacy and because it offered users more of a choice (something that television, though immediate, did not do as well).

Suddenly, printing news on paper and delivering it to homes – by which time the news itself was hours old – did not seem to fit into a world of instant communication.

But newspaper companies had billions of dollars invested in printing presses and impressive buildings. And they produced most of the journalism that the society depended on. And they delivered audiences to advertisers, which provided them money to operate. All of this could not simply go away or even change overnight. There had to be some kind of transition period

That is the state of journalism today.

Exactly how things will turn out economically is still one of the great unanswered questions of journalism. Newspaper companies have lost readers and advertisers – and thus revenue – at an alarming rate. Many have not been able to adjust to these new conditions quickly enough, and many of them are in danger of going out of business. Some already have. (The Rocky Mountain News in Denver stopped publication in 2009 after nearly 150 years of existence. Newspapers in Detroit, News Orleans and other cities are no longer printed daily..)

The recession of 2008-09 has pushed many newspaper companies to the brink financially and have accelerated many of changes that the field of journalism has been experiencing.

Those changes have not been just financial. The web has changed the way journalism is done in some important and fundamental ways. The web, unlike other media of print or broadcasting, has virtually unlimited capacity for content. A newspaper might cover a local collegiate football game and be able to run only one or two pictures of it; the newspaper's web site, however, might contain 100 or more pictures of the game.

The web also offers more flexibility in the form that information takes. It handles not only text and still images but also video and audio. Consequently, the journalist has to decide which form is best to present the information he or she has, and the journalist must be trained and experienced in using all forms of media.

The web has also introduced other changes in the process of journalism – changes that we will discuss throughout this course.

The most important of those changes is the interactivity that the web allows between the journalist and the consumers of news. In section 1.3 News consumers, we discussed the shifting metaphor of news from "news as product" to "news as conversation."

Journalists and news consumers are only beginning to understand this change and develop the full meaning of this concept. The "rules" governing news as conversation have not been written yet, and they are not likely to be settled any time soon. Chances are, the students who are reading this module and planning to become journalists will be among those who develop the new standards of journalism.

Because of the profound changes that are taking place in the profession, journalism today is an exciting field that is full of opportunities for hard-working and creative individuals. Society will continue to need journalism, just as it always has, but the form that it takes and the media that it uses will shift. Although careers in journalism are not predictable as they were a half century ago, undoubtedly there will be great opportunities for journalists to do important work and to make a good living while doing it.

Summary

• Journalism is an active and dynamic field today, just as it always was. We have many sources of news in print, broadcasting and the web.

• Many news organizations that were once large and profitable, especially newspapers, are now in financial difficulty.

• The web has changed the process of journalism and has undermined the old economic model.

• While the future is uncertain, there are undoubtedly many opportunities in journalism for those who are creative and willing to work hard.

Ask yourself:

A. The text says that the web has brought many changes to the process of journalism. Can you think of some changes that were not mentioned in the text? Hint: Think about deadlines from print and broadcasting versus deadlines for a web site. What would be the differences among those?

B. The text mentions four formats for information: text, pictures, audio and video. Which of the four do you think you are best at now? Which of these would you prefer to concentrate on? Why?

Discussion and activities:

A. Get a copy of today's local newspaper and then take a look at the newspaper's web site. What major differences do you see? Now take a look at the web site for a local television news station. What are the differences between that and the newspaper's web site?

B. This section talks about flexibility – that is, using text, pictures, video and audio. What does this mean for people training to be journalists?

C. The text of this section points out that the web has virtually unlimited capacity for content. At first, this may sound like a good thing. Are there down sides to it, however?

D. "Although careers in journalism are not predictable as they were a half century ago, ... " Discuss with your instructor and class what is meant by that statement.

References
Allan, Stuart. Online News: Journalism and the Internet. New York: Open University Press, 2006.

Stovall, James Glen. Web Journalism: Practice and Promise of a New Medium. Boston: Allyn and Bacon, 2004.

McGuire, Mary and Linda Stilborne, Melinda McAdams, Laurel Hyatt. The Internet Handbook for Writers, Researchers, and Journalists. New York: The Guilford Press, 2002.

Pew Project for Excellence in Journalism. The State of the News Media, 2009.

http://www.stateofthemedia.org/2009/index.htm

Advanced reading material

A Brief History of the Internet (The Internet Society)

http://www.isoc.org/internet/history/brief.shtml

Pew Internet and American Life Project

http://www.pewinternet.org/

Review questions

The major cause of change in journalism in the 1990s was

a few star reporters making lots and lots of money

the Internet

the mobile phone

The changes that have taken place in the profession of journalism in the last two decades have

reduced the opportunities for people who want to go into journalism

have increased the opportunities for people who want to go into journalism

have sent many journalism jobs overseas

7. The Beginning

Purpose
• To give students an overall sense of the history of journalism.

• To identify some of the major events and movements in the ancient history of journalism.

• To emphasize the importance of the progression of history and help students understand that where we are now is a product of what has happened before now.

Importance
Thinking of the history of journalism is vital to understanding its importance, concepts and process.

Four things are necessary for journalism to exist:

• information that people want or need to know;

• people who gather and disseminate that information;

• a technology with which to distribute the information;

• and an audience willing to receive the information.

Information has always been politically and economically valuable; at many times and in many places in history, it has also been considered dangerous.

Journalism is basic to the functioning of a society. Journalism is a means – the major means – of distributing information that society needs to exist and function. Consequently, as long as there have been societies that extended beyond a single family, there have been forms of information distribution and thus forms of journalism.

Modern journalism can trace some of its roots back to the Roman times of Caesar Augustus

One of the earliest civilized societies, the Sumerians who lived along the Tigris and Euphrates rivers (in what is now Iraq, Kuwait, Iran and Saudi Arabia) have left us some of the earliest forms of writing that we know about. The Sumerians wrote much – from daily merchant accounts to stories of their mythologies. They scratched symbols on moistened clay to keep records of what they had done and so they could refer to these records as they continued their lives. They even developed the concept of cylinder printing – the same process by which much of our printing is done today.

The Greeks ruled a diverse and far-flung empire that necessitated developing a means of sending information quickly long distances. Their "telegraph," as it were, was a series of signal fires and earthenware jars that were changed according to a pre-arranged set of rules.

As Greek power declined, the military forces of Rome acquired dominance over many of the known parts of the civilized world. Rome not only had to control an vast empire, but it also had to maintain a lively political and social system within the capital city. Both tasks require efficient means of information distribution, and it is from the Romans that we get the first hints of modern journalism. In 59 B.C., Emperor Julius Caesar ordered that an official account of the political news and acts of the Roman senate be published and distributed every day. This Acta Diurna (daily news) is thought by many to be the first newspaper. The publication contained more than the official acts of the government. It had news about fires, executions, and even the weather.

Duplication of books and "newspapers," such as they were, was accomplished mostly by hand rather than by any printing technology that we are familiar with today. Hand copying of manuscripts was an art and a skill that would remain in place for the next 1,500 years. Thus, daily news distribution in the form of writing was extremely limited and for the most part non-existent.

The development of the printing press in the 1450s in Germany was the great technological feat that gave us modern journalism.

Even with that, it took another 100 years for the first modern newspaper to come into existence. It was the Oxford Gazette, and it first appeared in Oxford, England, in 1655. It was independently owned but published with the consent of the government because it gave the government's view of the daily news.

Within the first 100 years of the history of the printing press, the technology spread rapidly through the continent. As that happened, Europeans – and particularly government officials – learned two things about current information:

• It could be valuable. People and organizations could and would use information to make decisions.

• It could be dangerous. As people got more information, they felt more empowered to make their own decisions rather than to follow the dictates of the government or the Church.

These two truths would have profound effects on the history of journalism.

Ask yourself:
A. Some people argue that history can tell us nothing. Argue the opposite point of view – that history can indeed tell us much about our lives.

B. What period of history fascinates you the most? Why?

C. Is there someone in your family who has spent a lot of time doing genealogical research? Talk to that person about why he or she is so interested in family history.

Discussion and activities:
A. Looking ahead: Read something about the Enlightenment, one of the most important events in human history. Human beings began to see themselves and the world around them differently. How would this change have affected the history and progress of journalism?

B. What do you know about Benjamin Franklin? Did you know that, in addition to all of his other accomplishments, he was the first great American journalist. Read something about his life to get familiar with some of his accomplishments as a journalist.

Summary
• Four things are necessary for journalism: information that people want or need to know; people who gather and disseminate that information; a technology with which to distribute the information; and an audience willing to receive the information.

• Hints of modern journalism can be found in all of the ancient societies, especially the Roman Empire, which at one point published a daily newspaper.

• The development of the printing press was the technological breakthrough that eventually gave us modern journalism.

While the future is uncertain, there are undoubtedly many opportunities in journalism for those who are creative and willing to work hard.

Review questions

Three of the four things that are need for journalism to exist are information, journalists, and technology. What is the fourth?

advertising

consensus

audience

In the early days of printing, government officials learned that journalism could be valuable and

safe

benign

dangerous

8. The News and 9/11

Purpose
To detail an example of when a historical event had a profound effect on journalism history.

Importance
Journalism has been called the "first rough draft of history," but we sometimes overlook the effect that historical events have in altering the course of journalism itself.

Anyone who recalls that day can remember the shock.

By all accounts from just about everywhere in America, it was a normal Tuesday in September. It was certainly that in New York City and Washington, D.C. The weather was clear and bright, and people were beginning their daily routines.

Then an airplane crashed into one of the twin towers of the World Trade Center. A few minutes later, this time with television cameras trained on the site, a second plane crashed into the other tower. Then a plane crashed into the side of the Pentagon, the nation's defense department headquarters, in Washington. A fourth plane full of airline passengers went down in a field in Pennsylvania.

Within two hours, both World Trade Center towers came crashing to the ground – a massively destructive event that simply had never happened before and that was hard to imagine.

The world soon became aware that

• these events had been deliberate and part of a terrorist attack on America;

• there was a massive loss of life;

• there was huge physical destruction;

- it was all happening in television, some of the events in real time.

The events of September 11, 2009, set off a decade of conflict and disruption that resulted in the invasion by American and allied forces into Afghanistan and Iraq; generalized conflict that pitted the culture and forces of the Western world against the Moslem religion; economic disruption that resulted in a world economic crisis in 2008 and 2009; political changes in the United States that led to the election of the first African-American president in 2008 and the displacement of the Republicans as the most dominant force in U.S. politics.

September 11 had another major effect: It changed the direction of journalism.

As with any major event in the last half century, America and the rest of the world watched the day's events unfold on television. They had been doing so since 1963 when, on a clear November day, John F. Kennedy, president of the United States, was killed by an assassin's rifle in Dallas, Texas.

That sudden, shocking event brought the country – and normal television broadcasting – to a halt for the next three days. It demonstrated the power of television to deliver news with impact and emotion in a way that, at that time, had no precedent.

Television was still doing that in 2001. But this time there was something different. There was the Internet.

And the Internet showed us the limitations of television, powerful as it is, as a news medium, because television can give us one and only one picture at a time. On September 11, 2001 – with so much news happening in so many places – we needed more than that. The Internet had given us the World Wide Web, and on September 11, the web grew up as a news medium.

Here's some of what happened on the web that day:

• From the time the second tower was hit (9:05 a.m.), the CNN web site got nine million hits an hour; that number increased to 19 million an hour by the next day. At that time, CNN had been getting about 14 million hits a day.

• The web portal Yahoo had 40 times its usual amount of traffic during the first hour after the attack on the trade center.

• MSNBC reported that in the first 24 hours of the disaster, 12.5 million people logged onto its site; the previous record had been 6.5 million on Nov. 8, the day after the disputed presidential election.

• People trying to check on friends in New York and Washington found phone lines clogged and resorted to email and instant messaging.

• Yahoo and other sites posted lists of victims and missing persons.

• Amazon.com, one of the major booksellers on the web, set up a donation for disaster relief for the Red Cross. By Saturday night, more than four days after the attack, the site had raised $5.7 million.

• To handle the increase in traffic, many web sites including the New York Times and CNN stripped off advertising and graphics in order to increase the loading speed for visitors.

The events of September 11 demonstrated the power of the web not only to deliver news and information but also to connect people with a speed and intimacy that they had never known before. What happened that day gave us an indication of what journalism would become over the next decade.

The changes that September 11 wrought in journalism have not yet played themselves out. In many ways, they have only begun, and it will be for a new generation of journalists – those who are reading this module – to give them definition.

(Part of this text was adapted from James Glen Stovall, Web Journalism: Practice and Promise of a New Medium, Allyn and Bacon, 2004. Used by permission of the author.)

Summary

• The events of September 11, 2001, altered not only the course of world history but also the history of the mass media.

• Television still dominated the news coverage of the events of September 11, but many people turned to the web for information. Just as importantly, many journalists used the web to disseminate information.

Ask yourself:

A. Do you or your fellow students remember the events of September 11, 2009? If so, write down your memories and share them with others.

Discussion and activities:

A. To understand how an important historic event can alter media history, find out as much as you can about the sinking of the Titanic in 1912 and the assassination of President John F. Kennedy in 1963.

9. Honesty

Purpose
To help students understand that honesty is not only a personal quality of the highest order for the journalist but for news organizations and the profession as a whole.

Importance
Honesty is the basis for quality communication. Journalists must be personally honest, but they must also work in an environment of trust with their audiences. This environment has not always existed, and journalists over many decades have had to create it.

A series of articles in the New York Sun in 1835 contained the following description:

The whole breadth of the northern extremity of the sea, which was about three hundred miles, having crossed our plane, we entered upon a wild mountainous region abounding with more extensive forests of larger trees than we had seen before — the species of which I have no good analogy to describe. In general contour they resembled our forest oak; but they were much more superb in foliage, having broad glossy leaves like that of the laurel, and tresses of yellow flowers which hung, in the open glades, from the branches to the ground. These mountains passed, we arrived at a region which filled us with utter astonishment. It was an oval valley, surrounded, except at narrow opening towards the south, by hills, red as the purest vermilion, and evidently crystallized; for wherever a precipitous chasm appeared — and these chasms were very frequent, and of immense depth — the perpendicular sections present conglomerated masses of polygon crystals, evenly fitted to each other, and arranged in deep strata, which grew darker in color as they descended to the foundations of the precipices. Innumerable cascades were bursting forth from the breasts of every one of these cliffs, and some so near their summits, and with such great force, as to form arches many yards in diameter. I never was so vividly reminded of Byron's simile, "the tale of the white horse in the Revolution." At the foot of this boundary of hills was a perfect zone of woods surrounding the whole valley, which was about eighteen or twenty miles wide, at its greatest breadth, and about thirty in length. Small collections of trees, of every imaginable kind, were scattered about the whole of the luxuriant area; and here our magnifiers blest our panting hopes with specimens of conscious existence.

In the shade of the woods on the south-eastern side, we beheld continuous herds of brown quadrupeds, having all the external characteristics of the bison, but more diminutive than any species of the bos genus in our natural history. . . .

What exotic place does this passage describe? Someplace in Africa? An unexplored region of America?

Neither. It purports to describe a region of the moon, as seen through a powerful telescope. The articles were written by Richard Adams Locke, a leading New York journalist of his day, and were spread out over a week. The most sensational revelations came late in the series when Locke describe human-like creatures that the powerful telescope had picked up.

The New York Sun at that point was less than two years old, but Locke's articles captured the attention of the city, and circulation soared to nearly 20,000 copies a day. After the series ended, discussion about it continued. Eventually, another newspaper revealed that the whole thing had been made up, but it still took a while for the Sun to admit that the articles were not true.

Despite that, the Sun's circulation continued to rise, and Locke's career as a journalist went on for several more years.

The Great Moon Hoax of 1835 – and possibly our reaction to it – shows us how different today's journalism is from that practiced in the early 19th century. Certainly, there are dishonest journalists today – people who willingly make things up and try to pass them off as the truth. But there are few, if any, instances where whole news organizations do that.

Unlike 1835, audiences expect news organizations to tell the truth.

And unlike 1835, information that is incorrect can be more easily checked and refuted, if necessary.

Finally, unlike 1835, honesty is a professional characteristic of value, not just a personal one.

Read more about the Great Moon Hoax here:

Museum of Hoaxes :
http://www.museumofhoaxes.com/moonhoax.html

Summary
• One of the most famous journalistic hoaxes is The Great Moon Hoax of 1835, written by Richard Adams Locke and published in the New York Sun. The series of stories told of the discoveries of plant life, animal life and even human-like creatures on the moon.

• The stories caused a sensation, but eventually the newspaper admitted that they were not true.

• The story of The Great Moon Hoax demonstrates that journalists and newspapers did not always have accuracy as their foremost consideration.

Discussion and activities:
A. How much do you believe the things you read and hear in the newspaper, on television or on the web?

B. Do you think something like the Great Moon Hoax could happen today? Why or why not?

C. Go to a good search engine such as Google and search for these terms: "Howard Hughes hoax" and "War of the Worlds." What did you find?

10. Photojournalism

Objective:

To allow students to gain an understanding of why photography is so important to our understanding of the world around us.

Importance:

The invention of photography in the 1830s changed the way people looked at their world and the way that ideas are shared and imprinted on our brains.

This invention had a profound effect on the way journalism is produced.

Photography brings to life *people, places, events* and other things that we would otherwise have trouble understanding. It has given us a common set of images with which to understand the environment that we do not personally experience.

Photographs – still images – are particularly effective in making a lasting impression on our brains. More than video – moving pictures – photographs allow us to reduce a person, place, event or subject to a manageable set of information that we can carry with us. The "pictures in our heads" have a great deal to do with the way we comprehend and interpret the things in our larger world.

For all of these reasons, photography is an important part of journalism. It, along with the words that we use, is a vital part of telling the story we have to tell. Photography gives the audience for journalism another dimension of information that they cannot get with words. It often gives life and form to the words that journalists use. It helps to entertain the audience as well as to deepen their understanding of the information in a story.

Photography is a way of impressing a story onto the brain of a reader.

Photojournalism became a primary part of journalism soon after the invention of photography in the 1830s. Cameras became a widely popular social phenomenon in the 1840s because they were new and people could have fun with them, but it took journalists less than a generation to recognize what a powerful tool they could be.

One of the first great photojournalists was Matthew Brady, a New York portrait photographer who traveled to many of the battlefields of the American Civil War in the 1860s to record what had happened there. Brady's images brought home to people who had stayed behind the starkness and horrors of war and helped change the way that people thought about war itself.

But photojournalism during the last part of the 19th century was not an easy thing to accomplish. The equipment required to take a picture was heavy, fragile and unreliable. Developing pictures from the film that had to be used was difficult and tedious. And even when the picture was taken and developed, there was no quick way of printing and distributing it widely because printing presses were developed to use type, not pictures.

These technical problems were gradually mitigated with the development of lighter and more portable cameras (although they were still massive machines compared to the tiny, hand-held cameras we have today). Film and the development process became more standardized, but it was never a particularly easy thing to get a print from film. Most importantly, the half-toning process for printing pictures allowed printers a quick way of getting sharp, clear and detailed images onto presses so they could be widely distributed.

By the middle of the 20th century, photography and photojournalism was an integral and important part of the journalistic process.

Because film photography and development had evolved into a highly precise and technical process, and because the skills to do this were ones that photographers had to hone over many years, photojournalists were slow to accept digital photography when it became widely available in the 1990s. Digital photography bypassed film and the development process (sometimes called "wet photography") by recording photos onto electronic disks and then using computers and software to produce the pictures.

Digital photography, from its beginnings, was definitely faster, and as quality equipment became much cheaper, it replaced film photography as the standard operating process for photojournalism. With today's cameras used in conjunction with the web, photos can be taken and transmitted around the world in a matter of seconds, where that process once took days or even weeks.

The digital revolution in photojournalism ushered in a more profound change in journalism and made it possible to take and produce pictures quickly. It brought photography within the reach of every journalist. While some people still consider themselves photojournalists, all journalists must consider themselves photographers. Photography should be a part of every story that every journalists covers.

That means:

All journalists should understand the basics of good picture taking.

Journalists should carry a camera and be familiar with its technical aspects.

Journalists should understand the software for editing photographs and should be very familiar with the process of preparing and uploading photos to the web.

Most importantly, journalists must integrate photography into their thinking about every story they cover.

Ask yourself:

D. Look at the photographs in the slideshow in this module. Each of the five photos will appear for 10 seconds. Which one do you remember? Describe it in as much detail as you can.

E. Why do you remember it?

Advanced reading material:

The Digital Journalist

Giles, Matthew, ed. Facing the World: Great Moments in Photojournalism. New York, N.Y. : H.N. Abrams, 2001.

Patterson, Freeman. Photography and the Art of Seeing. San Francisco : Sierra Club Books, 1989.

References:

Kobre, Kenneth and Betsy Brill. Photojournalism, The Professionals' Approach. 4th edition. Woburn, MA: Focal Press, 2000.

Frank Hoy. Photojournalism: The Visual Approach. Prentice Hall, 1993.

And check out the Tennessee Journalism Series' book of Photojournalism at

https://itunes.apple.com/us/book/photojournalism/id550459277?ls=1

11. The Intercollegiate Online News Network

The Intercollegiate Online News Network (ICONN) is an association of campus news websites, academic programs, individuals and professional organizations that have come together to encourage and promote web journalism education and to assist in the practice of online journalism on campus.

ICONN is the only organization devoted solely to the practice of collegiate online journalism.

Major activities of ICONN include

• Assisting the startup of campus news websites by providing a turnkey system – at no costs – for those who want to start news websites for their courses, departments or campuses;

• Providing server space and support – at no cost – for those sites;

• Offering training through in-person and online workshops to faculty and students who start or work on campus news websites;

• Giving those interested in web journalism education an independent organization to work with;

• Conducting an annual conference for those interested in collegiate web journalism;

• Providing a news service of collegiate news based on the content of the member sites;

• Developing an advertising system for those sites within the network to provide for long term sustainability

ICONN began in 2008 as an outgrowth of a grant and conference supported by the Scripps Howard Foundation. Conversations among academics revealed the need to rethink journalism education and the basic curriculum that we use to teach our students. One approach that was heavily discussed was to create campus news websites that would be owned and operated by faculty and academic programs rather than falling under the purview of student media. The availability of the technology to build news websites for programs and campuses was also a topic in these discussions. Finding a content management system that was inexpensive and easy to use emerged as a major problem to be solved.

ICONN set about solving this problem and now has a technical network and a WordPress-based content management system called JeffersonNet with which it provides start-up support for campus news websites. A faculty member, academic unit or campus organization that seeks to create a campus news website simply needs to declare itself in agreement with the basic goals of ICONN to become part of the network. ICONN does not charge a membership or any service fee for what it provides.

With the possibility of campus news websites starting up at various places around the country came the idea of tying those sites together in a news network. An ICONN news website needs to agree to share its originally produced content with other members of the network. With that agreement in place, ICONN sites have been informally sharing stories, photos, audio and video since 2009 through an individual copy and paste system. In 2011 with many new websites joining as members, we decided to take the next step in this concept and develop a news service we call the ICONN NewsStream. We are currently in the middle of both the technical and conceptual development of the NewsStream idea.

Another logical outgrowth of the network idea was to develop an advertising service for the network. Such a service would be designed to sell national advertising to sites throughout the network; regional advertising to selected sites within the network; and local advertising to individual websites. Revenue from this service would be based on page views and would be divided among the advertising service handling these operations, ICONN, and the individual sites. The ICONN advertising service is also under technical and conceptual development.

ICONN held its first annual conference in January 2009 in Knoxville with about 50 students and faculty in attendance and more than a dozen colleges and universities represented. A second annual conference was held in January 2010 also in Knoxville, and our third annual conference was in March 2011 in Athens, GA. We held our fourth annual conference in Nashville, TN, in April 2012.

At the end of the academic year of 2012-2013, there were more than 40 campus news websites that are part of the network. Some are within ICONN's JeffersonNet technical system, and some exist on their own and participate in ICONN's membership and news services.

ICONN has developed a scholastic arm, the Interscholastic Online News Network (ISONN), that offers many of these same services to high schools and high school journalism teachers. Currently, there are more than 20 high school news websites that are a part of the ISONN JeffersonNet system.

How to establish an ICONN/ISONN website

If you are interested in establishing a website within the ICONN network, you can do this quickly and with relatively few steps. The first thing to do is to reserve a domain name.

You can use any of the suffixes available to you for your name: .com, .org, .info, .us, etc. If you do not have a preferred service for registration, we recommend using GoDaddy.com.

When you have reserved your name, you should email Jim Stovall at jgstovall at gmail.com.

Next, you will need to change the DNS servers. This sound technical, but it's really very simple. Go into the account where you have reserved the name and find the DNS servers that are listed. Change those to the following: dns1.stabletransit.com and dns2.stabletransit.com

If you are using GoDaddy, here are the specific steps:

1. Log in to your Account Manager.

2. In the My Products section, select Domain Manager.

3. Select the domain name(s) you want to modify.

4. From (Nameservers), select Set Nameservers.

5. Select the following option: I have specific nameservers for my domains

6. Enter the following two nameservers: dns1.stabletransit.com and dns2.stabletransit.com.

This change may take a few minutes or even several hours to go into effect. Meanwhile, if you let us know that you have done this, we can establish your site on our end. When that happens, we will send you an email "inviting" you to join the site as an administrator. The email will have a confirmation link and a password.

Once you confirm, and enter the backend of your site, you should click on your name in the upper right corner. That will take you to your account page. At the bottom of that page, you should change your password to something that you will remember.

That's it.

Your site is up and running, and you can start with the other operations described in this handbook.

12. BONUS CHAPTER: The First Amendment

The following chapter is an abridged version of The First Amendment, on of the titles in the Tennessee Journalism Series.

The First Amendment to the U.S. Constitution protects five important freedoms: religion, speech, press, assembly and petition.

Religion

Many Americans have their history wrong. They believe that the first European settlers of this nation came to America because they believed in the right to practice religion and worship freely.

Actually, many of them came because they wanted to practice their religion freely. They did not care about the right of people outside their own groups to observe a different set of beliefs.

During the colonial years there was as much religious intolerance and state supported religion practice as there was in England or any place else in Europe.

But that began to change in the late 18th century, particularly through the writing and efforts of Thomas Jefferson, who challenged the government's role in religious observance.

Freedom of religion today

Today, through many events and court cases, we have developed some fundamental understandings about what the words of the First Amendment mean (sometimes referred to as the 'establishment clause'):

Individuals have the right to believe, practice religion, and worship as they see fit.

Individuals are not required to support any religion or religious organization.

The government cannot establish or support any religious organization.

The government must remain neutral in dealing with religious organizations and beliefs.

Even with these fundamental understandings, there are still many controversies and issues surrounding the First Amendment's guarantee of freedom of religion and of the state neutrality toward religion. For instance, consider these:

– prayer in schools

– creationism

– posting the Ten Commandments in government buildings

– requiring the recitation of the Pledge of Allegiance in schools

– blue laws

– putting Christmas decorations on public property

The list could go on.

Speech
If the First Amendment means anything, we believe, it means that we have the right to speak our minds — to say what we think, right?

That's correct.

But it wasn't always so.

In the early days of the Republic, laws were passed that protected the president and administration from criticism.

Many states had laws restricting the freedom of speech, especially in the South where is was against the law to advocate abolition (freeing slaves). Yet Americans have always enjoyed debating the issues of the day. They like to argue, disagree, and even diss one another. From colonial days Americans have sought solutions to social, economic and political problems by vigorous and animated discussion. Sometimes those discussions have turned violent. More often than not, however, the discussions have ultimately resulted in commonly agreed upon solutions and principles.

Despite its halting beginning, "free speech" proved its value more than once, and the concept is now deeply embedded in the American psyche.

Still, as much as we honor free speech, we are sometimes not very careful in preserving it. Our tendency to censor speech that is disturbing or disagreeable — or that doesn't agree with what seems to be the majority opinion — sometimes gets the best of us. We also have a tendency to think that if we limit speech in certain ways and on certain topics, we can solve some pressing social problem. Particularly during national crises, we tend to believe that if we can just stop people from saying certain things, our nation will be more secure.

When we do this, however, we are defying our own best instincts and a logic that experience teaches again and again. We can never successfully keep people from saying what they believe in, from believing whatever they choose, and from expressing those beliefs publicly. Other societies try doing this, and eventually they explode.

People do not like to be told that they cannot say something.

Neither do we.

Our job as Americans is to protect free speech wherever it is threatened. We should constantly be on guard against the thinking that restricting speech will somehow make us a better society. We should preserve our unique place in the world as a society who values its individual citizens and protects them even when they say or do things that are not popular.

Press
This part of the First Amendment

> *'. . . or of the press . . .'*

has generated a great deal of debate and much litigation throughout the history of the Republic.

Just what did the founders of the Republic mean by that? How have we interpreted that phrase since it was originally written?

Answers to those questions have filled many volumes, but generally we believe that the government should not censor printed material; that it should not exercise prior restraint (preventing something from being printed or distributed) on publications; and that it should not hinder the distribution of printed material.

In journalism, this freedom extends to the practice of journalism itself. Reporters should be able to gather information. Government bodies – courts, legislative units, boards, etc. – should operate in the open. Government records should be available to all citizens who request them. In some cases, reporters are protected from disclosing their sources because of this clause in the First Amendment.

Two important areas where the freedom to publish is limited are: libel or defamation; and copyright and trademark.

Libel or defamation

Libel – the concept that words can harm a person's reputation – is an ancient principle of common law. A person's reputation has value, and when that value is diminished, a person can seek redress from the courts.

Yet there is the First Amendment, which says society has value in being able to speak freely. How do we resolve this conflict?

Despite the language of the First Amendment, libel laws exist and are, occasionally, enforced. Journalists must be careful about libel.

Modern defamation laws say that to win a libel case, you must prove

• publication (more than just two people have to see/hear it)

• identification (can the person defamed be identified)

• defamation (did the words have potential to do real damage)

• fault (was there negligence or some mitigation)

• harm (is there provable damage)

Defenses against defamation

Statute and case law provide some strong defenses for people facing libel actions:

• truth – powerful defense (society values truth)

• qualified privilege – is the situation one that relieves people of libel responsibility? Reporters depend on the concept of qualified privilege to report public affairs. For instance, they may report the arrest of a person who ultimately is declared innocent of a crime.

• absolute privilege – Some instances, such as a legislator speaking in a meeting of the legislature, can say anything he or she wishes without regard to libel laws.

• statute of limitations – Courts do not like old cases, particularly in civil matters. Many states have a statue of limitations provision that says a libel suit must be filed within two years of the alleged libel.

• Constitutional privilege – This privilege protects news media from suits by public officials and public figures. It comes from a 1964 decision, New York Times v. Sullivan. The results of this case make virtually impossible for any well known figure to recover damages in a libel action.

Still, the threat of the costs of litigation are real, and journalists should be careful to avoid them if possible.

Copyright

The freedom to write and publish is not unlimited.

One area in which that freedom is limited is that of copyright and trademarks, which are part of a larger area of law known as intellectual property. People who create what we might term generally as "intellectual property" – books, musical works, art, sculpture, articles, poems, etc. – have some protection in the way that those works are used by others. If you draw a picture or write a poem, that picture or poem is yours (at least for a limited amount of time), and no one else can reprint it without your permission.

There are things that copyright does not cover, however.

Facts cannot be copyrighted. Let's say you are the only writer covering your high school basketball game, and you write a story about it for the high school paper. Another publication can take the facts that you have described – the details of the game, the score, etc. – and use them in its description of the game.

That publication, however, cannot use your account of the game. The expression of facts can be copyrighted, but the facts themselves cannot.

Like facts, ideas cannot be copyrighted, but the expression of those ideas can. For instance, you can paint a picture of a tree, and that painting will be copyrighted. Someone else can paint a picture of the same tree. That's OK, as long as they do not use your painting.

The protection of a copyright is limited in two important ways. One is that it does not last forever. Currently, copyrights last for the life of the creator, plus 70 years. If the copyright is owned by a corporation, the copyright lasts longer. A copyright does not last forever. At some point, all creative works become part of the "public domain"; that is, everyone owns them. Consequently, the works of William Shakespeare, for instance, are in the public domain, and Shakespeare can be quoted at length without anyone's permission.

The second limitation of copyright is through the concept of fair use. This concept has been developed to encourage the dissemination of ideas and information without either putting a great burden on the user or infringing on the rights of the creator of the work. Fair use means that in certain limited circumstances, a copyrighted work – or more likely, some portion of it – may be used without the permission of the holder of the copyright.

Courts have looked at four things in considering what is fair use:

– the nature of the copyrighted material – how much effort it took to produce it;

– the nature of the use – for instance, material used in an educational setting for educational purposes is more likely to be thought of as fair use;

– the extent of the use – how much of the copyrighted material is used, just a few words or a whole passage;

– commercial infringement – most importantly, how much does the use hurt the commercial value of the work.

Unless material is being used in a very limited way, you should always get permission to use copyrighted material. Holders of copyright can be very aggressive about enforcing their copyrights, and the unauthorized user of a copyright can be fined substantially. Many people in education believe that they can use any material in any way they wish, and it will be considered fair use. That is not the case. Educators are bound by copyright laws as much as anyone else.

Note: Material on the Internet has as much copyright protection as anything else. Some people believe that whatever is on a web site is in the public domain, and that is not the case. Just because material is easy to access does not mean that it does not have copyright protection.

Trademark

A special protection for the commercial use of words, phrases and symbols is trademark.

Many companies go to great lengths to protect their trademarks because that is how the public identifies their products. What if, for example, a shoe company named Nuke started using the Nike symbol, the swoosh, on its shoes? Consumers might become confused about what product to buy, and Nike, which holds a trademark on the swoosh, might be hurt by that.

Assembly
The First Amendment guarantees that people can get together – peaceably – and talk about whatever they want to discuss.

Courts have almost always recognized that governments have the power to regulate time and place of assembly when the public's safety and convenience is an issue.

But governments are prevented from saying to a group of people that they cannot meet when the reason for their meeting is legal.

According to the First Amendment Center:

First Amendment freedoms ring hollow if government officials can repress expression that they fear will create a disturbance or offend. Unless there is real danger of imminent harm, assembly rights must be respected.

About the picture:

Before 1920, most women in the United States could not vote. In the 19th century, they had few legal rights at all, and the social customs against women being seen in public unless they were with another woman or accompanied by a man were strict and unacceptable by today's standards. When women starting petitioning for the right to vote in the early part of the 20th century, they began holding parades, exercising their right to assembly. Here is the beginning of the Washington Suffrage Parade of 1913, a significant event in the history of the suffrage movement. For more information on this parade and its effect on the eventual passage of the Nineteenth Amendment, go to Seeing Suffrage (http://seeingsuffrage.com).

Petition
When an individual

calls the tax assessor's office to complain that property taxes have gone up too much,

attends a town meeting public officials and policies are questioned,

joins a legal street demonstration to gain publicity for their cause,

pays a lobbyist or joins a group that pays someone to go to Washington or the state capital to argue for a cause, then that person is petitioning 'the Government for a redress of grievances' – a right protected by the First Amendment.

The right to petition the government was very much on the minds of the Founding Fathers. As colonists, they had asked King George III and the government in London many times to pay attention to what they wanted. Mostly, the people in England ignored them.

So, when it came time to write the Declaration of Independence, they included the following in their reasons for declaring independence:

"In every state of these Oppressions We have Petitioned for Redress in the most humble terms: Our repeated Petitions have been answered only by repeated injury."

Governments in the U.S. do not have to agree with the petitioner or do what he or she asks. But they must listen.

And they cannot retaliate against the petitioner for asking.

Compared to the other parts of the First Amendment, the right to petition the government has not generated much litigation or attention among scholars over the years. Perhaps, according to Adam Newton, writing for the First Amendment Center, that is because it continues to work so well. The petition clause is the tacit assumption in constitutional analysis, the primordial right from which other expressive freedoms arise. Why speak, why publish, why assemble against the government at all if such complaints will only be silenced?

About the picture:

Mary Gertrude Fendall (left) and Mary Dubrow (right) standing outside what is likely National Woman's Party headquarters, holding between them a large sign containing text of a Resolution Addressed to Senator Edward J. Gay with a long unrolled sheet of paper, presumably signatures on a petition, laying on the ground in front of them. The sign was in support of the Nineteenth Amendment, which would have given women the right to vote. The sign mentions mentions that "President Woodrow Wilson has urged the passage of the Federal Suffrage amendment before the Senate of the United States and again recently before the whole Congress of the United States as a necessary War and Reconstruction Measure . . ." Wilson first publicly declared his support for the amendment on Jan. 9, 1918. He asked the Senate to pass the amendment as a war measure on Sept. 30, 1918. The amendment was passed in the House on May 21, 1919, and in the Senate on June 4, 1919. Library of Congress photos, circa 1918-1919.

History

The First Amendment grew ouy of four concepts of behavior of human beings in society (as identified by Teeter, Le Duc, and Loving):

marketplace of ideas

individual fulfillment

safety valve

self-governance

Each of the concepts is important for an understanding
of why people in the 18th century — the time when
America earned its independence from Great Britain and
adopted the Constitution — believed in the notion of
freedom of speech.

The marketplace of ideas is based on the concept that no
one person or entity knows the truth that can be applied
to every action of mankind. Since no human has the
authority to say what is right or wrong or true or not
true, ideas must be expressed and tested. The famous
English author John Milton gave voice to the
marketplace of ideas (although he did not use that term),
and many in the 18th century followed his line of
thinking. Simply put, the concept is that if everyone can
express his or her ideas, the truth will eventually
emerge.

Individual fulfillment means that all people have
potential to become more than they are. As humans,
they need the freedom to express themselves and to try
to expand and improve their character and productivity.
By doing this, they are of benefit to the entire society.
People can define themselves through their individual
expressions.

The idea of freedom of speech as a safety valve means
that individuals can express opposition to authority
without punishment, and this — in the long run — has
a calming effect on the political society. If people know
that at the very least they can speak and be heard, they
are less likely to rebel against the whole structure of the
state.

Finally, free speech is the basis of self governance. No
society can claim to have its people self governing if it
does not allow free expression of ideas.

These ideas were floating around and much debated
when America won its independence from Great Britain
in the 1780s. A great deal of free speech had already
been practiced by the Founding Fathers as they were

making war against Britain and as they were setting up their own government, so individual rights did not seem like a critical issue.

But as Americans debated the ratification of a new Constitution in 1787 and 1788, many prominent people — people such as Patrick Henry and Samuel Adams — opposed the Constitution because they believed that it would concentrate too much power in the hands of two few people. Individual liberties — the right to speak and to assemble, for instance — would be threatened by the newly powerful centralized authorities.

To counter those arguments, proponents of the Constitution promised that, once the document was ratified and put into place, they would support a set of amendments that would guarantee the rights about which the opponents were concerned. James Madison, who had been a chief architect of the Constitution itself, took the lead in drafting these amendments, which eventually became known as the Bill of Rights.

The First Amendment is the first of 10 of these amendments. Some deal with individual liberties. Others deal with how the government must handle individuals accused of a crime. Still others restrict government action in certain areas.

The First Amendment is not first because the Founding Fathers considered it the most important one. The historical record indicates that they clearly did not. Still, the fact that it is first has invested it with much value. What is means exactly is still a matter of vigorous debate.

The politics of the First Amendment
The First Amendment, as Professor Teeter says in the video related to this section (see the end of the section), is "the chance product of political expediency." (He's quoting Leonard Levy, another First Amendment scholar.) How did that happen?

James Madison was the chief author of the new Constitution that had been put forth by those wanting to form a strong central government in 1787. As such, Madison became one of the leaders in arguing for its ratification. The Constitution was the product of weeks of delicate compromise on many of its points, and Madison feared that any changes to it would destroy its chance for passage.

That's exactly what the opponents of the Constitution hoped, and they began complaining that the Constitution did not protect individuals from the powers of government to take away civil liberties, such as freedom of speech, freedom of the press and the right to trial by jury. This debate took place in just about every state that considered the Constitution but it was conducted fiercely in Virginia, Madison's home state. Opponents were led by Patrick Henry, the popular orator of the Revolution and a man still active in politics. Henry and other feared a powerful central government.

Sitting on the fence in this debate were the Virginia Baptists and other religious groups who had been fighting against the established and official religion of the Anglican church. Baptists were persuaded by these argument — especially by the lack of separation of church and state.

This put them and James Madison in an awkward position. Madison and the Baptists had been strong allies in the fight against an established church. Now, Madison appeared to be abandoning that principle with his support for this new Constitution.

In truth, Madison did not think that these rights needed to be protected by the new Constitution, and he feared that adding them would upset the fine balance he had struck to complete the Constitution to begin with. But he recognized and understood the concerns of his friends, the Baptists. He also knew that without their support, it would be unlikely that Virginia would ratify the Constitution. And if Virginia, the largest state among the original 13 colonies, did not do so, the Constitution itself would not be ratified.

So, Madison promised to support a bill of rights that would be added to the Constitution after it had been ratified and the first government had been established. He promised to run for Congress and then to do what he could to introduce the necessary amendments. That stance put Madison in the position of admitting that there was something lacking about the Constitution that he so ardently supported. Still, he did what was necessary and was able to persuade the Baptists and other concerned religious groups to his side.

The Constitution was ultimately ratified, and the new government was put in place.

Madison was elected to the Congress but initially found little support among his colleagues for immediately amending the Constitution before it had had a chance to work. Still, he had made a promise, and he used his massive intellect and political skill to keep that promise

As historian Forrest Church has written:

His (Madison's) authorship of the First Amendment constitutes perhaps his most abiding legacy. Acting on the crucial impetus provided by his Baptist constituents, he etched church-state separate and freedom of conscience into the American code.

For more on the ratification battles over the U.S. Constitution, see the Teaching American History website.

The First Amendment in the 19th and early 20th centuries
By the early 1790s, the First Amendment, along with the other nine amendments that constituted the Bill of Rights, had been ratified — and seemingly quickly forgotten. During the single term of the John Adams presidency (1797 - 1800), Congress passed and the president signed the Alien and Sedition Acts that outlawed criticism of the president and those in power.

Republicans such as Thomas Jefferson and James Madison — in opposition to the Federalists — could do little about these acts. The Supreme Court had not yet established itself as the body that could review laws passed by Congress for their constitutionality, so there was at that point no check on congressional power. The acts themselves were ineffective in stifling criticism of the president, and fortunately, they expired after two years. By that time, Thomas Jefferson had been elected president, and the Federalists would never return to power. The Alien and Sedition Acts stained the Adams presidency, and they made heroes out of those they meant to persecute.

The First Amendment and the other parts of the Bill of Rights were meant to restrain Congress. People of the early republic saw their power and intent as limited. States and state constitutions were still the source of governmental power that Americans recognized as most important. Recall that the First Amendment begins with the words: "Congress shall make no law . . ." This phrase was deliberate and taken seriously by the people of the time. Congress could not make laws, but states certainly could.

In addition, we need to understand that the greatest concern of those who composed the First Amendment was religious liberty and the free exercise of religious practices — not free expression. Madison, Jefferson and their allies wanted to prevent the new government from establishing an official church — not guaranteeing free speech or a free press. They wanted to build a "wall of separation" between the government and the church.

In this, they were highly successful. Religious liberty and the free exercise of religion — without interference from the government – became an established principle of the nation. It is one that remains in effect today, so much so that we often take it for granted.

But the idea of freedom of expression had a tougher time.

The chief and abiding political and moral issue facing American in the first half of the 19th century was slavery. Slaves had been in America for 300 years by that time, and slavery had worked its way into the social, political and economic system. As tobacco and cotton — particularly cotton — grew in importance, slavery as a means of producing these products also strengthened.

The emotional and political costs were enormous.

Whites, especially those in the South where slavery existed and grew, lived in constant fear that slaves would one day rise up in bloody revolt. Those fears were not groundless. Slaves in the newly formed nation of Haiti had done just that, and every Southern plantation resident had nightmares that the same thing would happen on their land, even though they might fool themselves into thinking that their slaves were happy and contented.

Northerners shared many of those fears, and because their economic systems did not depend so much of cotton and tobacco, Northern states were able to free themselves slowly from the slavery system. Still, the fear of the possibility of a slave revolt was national.

Consequently, those who advocated freedom for slaves --emancipationists and abolitionists — were not welcome in many places. Southern states passed laws against the printing and distribution of abolitionist newspapers. They also outlawed the open advocacy of emancipation or abolition. In some cases, newspaper editors who wrote about such things had their presses destroyed, were run out of town, or in a few tragic instances, killed. Clearly, these situations offend our 21st century ideas of what the First Amendment should mean, but most people of the time did not view the First Amendment in this fashion.

One man who did was a Kentucky newspaper editor named Cassius Marcellus Clay. Clay had come from a slave-holding family in Kentucky but during his college days at Yale had been persuaded that slavery was wrong. He became an emancipationist, someone who advocated the gradual freeing of slaves.

(Abolitionists favored immediate freedom for slaves.) Clay was stubborn and tough. He was criticized harshly for his stance and physically attacked several times for what he wrote about slavery.

Clay was one of the few men of the 19th century to say that the First Amendment to the Constitution should protect people like him from any government intrusion.

The nation did not hear or heed Clay, and those who advocated unpopular ideas were subjected to legal and extra-legal pressures to conform or remain silent. During the Civil War, Lincoln and his administration brought government power to bear against those they felt were endangering the war efforts.

The one bright spot in the 19th century for civil liberties came in 1868 when the nation ratified the 14th Amendment, which said that states could not deprive people of liberty or property without resorting to "due process of law" and could not deny people the "equal protection" of the law. This amendment was put in place to assure that freed slaves would be given their full rights in states where slavery has previously be prevalent. This was clearly a check on state power and an assertion that the U.S. Constitution was the ultimate law of the land. It was another 50 years before this idea — that states had to be subject to the will of the federal constitution — took hold in any meaningful sense. When it did, in a 1925 Supreme Court ruling, it changed the entire balance of legal power in the United States and set us on the road to our modern thinking about First Amendment protections.

Meanwhile, America endured several national crises, including what was then known as the Great War (1914 - 1918). We call it World War I today. It was a time, more than any other in the nation's history, when the American government, under the direction of Woodrow Wilson, strayed from the principle of protecting free expression.

In 1917, the year America entered the war, Congress passed the Espionage Act which made it a crime "to willfully cause or attempt to cause insubordination, disloyalty, mutiny, or refusal of duty, in the military or naval forces of the United States," or to "willfully obstruct the recruiting or enlistment service of the United States."

The next year saw passage of the Sedition Act, which outlawed spoken or printed criticism of the U.S. government, the Constitution or the flag.

The Wilson administration was vigorous in using these laws and other means to suppress dissent. Part of the woman suffrage movement — the Woman Political Party led by Alice Paul — were particularly irritating to the administration. Despite America's entry into the war, members of the NWP continued to picket the White House, demanding that Wilson support suffrage at home while he was touting the expansion of democracy abroad.

The women picketers were arrested for "obstructing sidewalk traffic" and hauled off to jail. At first, their sentences were relatively light (two to six days in many cases), and the administration hoped the arrests would discourage future demonstrations. The opposite occurred.

Women continued to picket the White House, and the signs they carried grew more pointed. When they were rearrested, they were given longer sentences. The women asked to be treated as political prisoners, a status they were denied. They then went on hunger strikes. Prison officials, with the administration's approval, subjected the women to forced feeding, a torture process that kept the women alive but weakened and injured them.

Once out of jail, the suffragists continued to picket the White House and tell the story of what happened to them at the hands of government officials — all for non-violently demanding their political rights. The picketing and protests continued after the war and up until the passage of the 19th Amendment that gave women the right to vote.

The treatment the suffragists received was not as harsh that meted out to those charged and convicted under the Espionage and Sedition Acts. Some people spent years in prison for the crime of protesting the nation's involvement in the Great War — violating the rights to speech and petition that the First Amendment was supposed to protect.

Courts were of little use in protecting these rights. The Supreme Court on numerous occasions had the opportunity to check the administration's actions but failed to do so.

As America came out of the war, many people were disturbed by the heavy-handedness of the Wilson administration in suppressing dissent. They believed that America was in danger of losing its way as the beacon of free societies and that more attention should be paid to actively protecting civil liberties than to simply saying that "Congress shall make no law . . ."

This change in attitude did not occur all at once. Rather, it was a step-by-step process that began with the Supreme Court ruling in Gitlow v. New York in 1925. In that decision, for the first time, the Court said that because of the 14th Amendment, Constitutional protections, such as those in the First Amendment, applied to state actions. This decision opened the door for a wide variety of other decisions during the next 40 years that strengthened protections guaranteed by the Bill of Rights.

First Amendment Videos

Gitlow v. New York

Videos of Dr. Dwight Teeter discussing various aspects of the First Amendment and how it developed can be found at these links:
https://vimeo.com/9852487
https://vimeo.com/9754284
https://vimeo.com/9748541
https://vimeo.com/9823451
https://vimeo.com/9772215

Timeline of First Amendment events of the 19th century

The 19th century witnesses a Supreme Court hostile to many claims of freedom of speech and assembly. Fewer than 12 First Amendment cases come before the court between 1791 and 1889, according to First Amendment scholar Michael Gibson. This is due to the prevailing view among federal judges that the Bill of Rights does not apply to the states.

1801

Congress lets the Sedition Act of 1798 expire, and President Thomas Jefferson pardons all person convicted under the Act. The act had punished those who uttered or published "false, scandalous, and malicious" writings against the government.

1836

The U.S. House of Representatives adopts gag rules preventing discussion of antislavery proposals. The House repeals the rules in 1844.

1859

John Stuart Mill publishes the essay "On Liberty." The essay expands John Milton's argument that if speech is free and the search for knowledge unfettered, then eventually the truth will rise to the surface.

1863

Gen. Ambrose Burnside of the Union Army orders the suspension of the publication of the Chicago Times on account of repeated expression of disloyal and incendiary sentiments. President Lincoln rescinds Burnside's order three days later.

1864

By order of President Lincoln, Gen. John A. Dix, a Union commander, suppresses the New York Journal of Commerce and the New York World and arrests the newspapers' editors after both papers publish a forged presidential proclamation purporting to order another draft of 400,000 men. Lincoln withdraws the order to arrest the editors and the papers resume publication two days later.

1868

The 14th Amendment to the Constitution is ratified. The amendment, in part, requires that no state shall "deprive any person of life, liberty, or property, without due process of law; nor deny to any person within its jurisdiction the equal protection of the laws."

1873

Anti-obscenity reformer Anthony Comstock successfully lobbies Congress to pass the Comstock Law. This is the first comprehensive anti-obscenity statute enacted at the federal level. The law targets the "Trade in and Circulation of, obscene literature and Articles for immoral use" and makes it illegal to send any "obscene, lewd or lascivious" materials or any information or "any article or thing" related to contraception or abortion through the mail.

Source: The First Amendment Center

Chapter sources

Dwight Teeter, Don Le Duc, Bill Loving. The Law of Mass Communication (9th ed). New York: Foundation Press, 1998.

Forrest Church, So Help Me God: The Founding Fathers and the First Great Battle Over Church and State. Orlando: Harcourt, 2007.

Christopher M. Duncan. The Anti-Federalists and Early American Political Thought. DeKalb, Ill. : Northern Illinois University Press, 1995

The Author

The author of this book is James Glen Stovall. He is a professor of journalism at the University of Tennessee and author of, among other books, Writing for the Mass Media, a media writing text that is now in its eighth edition. He is the executive director of the Intercollegiate Online News Network. (Yes, that's actually him in the picture; he keeps bees, among other things.)

Made in the USA
Lexington, KY
30 January 2014